MAD LIBS
WORKBOOK
GRADE 4 READING

written by Wiley Blevins

MAD LIBS
An Imprint of Penguin Random House LLC, New York

Mad Libs format and text copyright © 2021 by Penguin Random House LLC. All rights reserved.

Mad Libs concept created by Roger Price & Leonard Stern

Cover illustration by Scott Brooks
Interior illustrations by Scott Brooks, Gareth Conway, and Tim Haggerty

Designed by Dinardo Design

Published by Mad Libs,
an imprint of Penguin Random House LLC, New York.
Manufactured in China

Visit us online at www.penguinrandomhouse.com.

ISBN 9780593222843
3 5 7 9 10 8 6 4 2

WORKBOOK

— INSTRUCTIONS —

MAD LIBS WORKBOOK is a game for kids who don't like games! It is also a review of the key reading skills for Grade 4. It has both skill practice pages and fun story pages.

RIDICULOUSLY SIMPLE DIRECTIONS:

At the top of each story page, you will find four columns of words, each headed by a symbol. Each symbol represents a type of word, such as a noun (naming word) or a verb (action word). The symbols are:

NOUN	VERB	ADJECTIVE	ADVERB
★	➡	☺	?

MAD LIBS WORKBOOK is fun to play by yourself, but you can also play it with friends! To begin, look at the story on the page below. When you come to a blank space in the story, look at the symbol that appears underneath. Then find the same symbol on this page and pick a word that appears below the symbol. Put that word in the blank space, and cross out the word, so you don't use it again. Continue doing this throughout the story until you've filled in all the spaces. Finally, read your story aloud and laugh!

EXAMPLE:

NOUN	VERB	ADJECTIVE	ADVERB
★	➡	☺	?
~~alien~~	dancing	~~purple~~	happily
~~elephant~~	~~twirling~~	~~spotted~~	carefully
orangutan	tiptoeing	angry	~~frantically~~

We spotted an _____alien_____ under the desk. It was _____spotted_____ and
                    ★   ☺
_____twirling_____ around. I _____frantically_____ left the room and fainted in the
        ➡   ?
hallway. I woke up being stared at by a _____purple_____ _____elephant_____ .
                                             ☺   ★

QUICK REVIEW

In case you haven't learned about phonics yet, here is a quick review:

There are five **VOWELS**: *a*, *e*, *i*, *o*, and *u*. Each vowel has a short sound and a long sound. The long sound of a vowel says its name. Sometimes the consonants *w* and *y* act as vowels when they are in vowel teams, such as *ow* (snow) and *ay* (play).

All the other letters are called **CONSONANTS**.

A **DIGRAPH** is two or more letters that together make a new sound, such as *sh* (shop) and *ch* (chin).

A **SYLLABLE** is a word part. It has one vowel sound, such as *rain* or *rain/bow*.

A **PREFIX** is a word part added to the beginning of a word, such as *un* in *unhappy*. It changes the word's meaning.

A **SUFFIX** is a word part added to the end of a word, such as *s* (bugs), *ing* (jumping), *ed* (stomped), and *ful* (playful).

In case you have forgotten about the parts of speech, here is a quick review:

A **NOUN** is the name of a person, place, or thing. *Lion*, *classroom*, and *stove* are nouns.

A **VERB** is an action word. *Skate*, *jump*, and *scream* are verbs.

An **ADJECTIVE** describes a person, place, or thing. *Soft*, *fluffy*, and *square* are adjectives.

An **ADVERB** is a word that tells more about a verb or adjective. It can tell how, when, where, or how much. *Slowly*, *carefully*, *eagerly*, and *really* are adverbs.

A **PRONOUN** takes the place of a noun in a sentence, such as *I*, *you*, *he*, *she*, *it*, *we*, and *they*.

Closed Syllables

A **closed syllable** ends in a consonant and has a short vowel sound. Knowing this can help you chunk and read longer words.

<u>**mid**</u>/dle   <u>**ab**</u>/sent

Add the missing **closed syllable**.

__ __ __ bit

__ __ __ __ ken

__ __ __ ton

cac __ __ __

__ __ __ __ __ kin

pen __ __ __

__ __ __ ket

__ __ __ __ __ tor

__ __ __ pass

ther __ __ __

NOUN	VERB	ADJECTIVE	ADVERB
★	➡	😊	?
magnet	defending	scenic	happily
cabin	cleaning	plastic	carefully
pumpkin	giggling at	zigzag	frantically
kitten	honoring	rectangular	quietly

Lake Patrol

Ranger Robin's job is to patrol the state park. One morning, Ranger Robin was

_____ checking the park's _____ lake. Many
           ?   😊

tourists liked to visit the _____ there. Some came for the swimming.
                                    ★

Some came to picnic. Others came to _____ boat and fish. The clean
                                              ?

waters of the park were well-known. They were protected by the park rules and state

laws. It was her job to make sure people were _____ the rules. The
                                                        ➡

park's _____ was beautiful in the sunrise. The pink
              ★

sunlight looked _____ as it softly colored the lake
                       😊

water. Ranger Robin felt content _____ this
                                          ➡

stunning resource.

Open Syllables

An **open syllable** ends in a vowel and has a long vowel sound. Knowing this can help you chunk and read longer words.

<u>**ze**</u>/bra   <u>**si**</u>/lent

Add the missing **open syllable**.

__ __ by

__ __ lip

__ __ ble

__ __ __ zen

__ pron

__ __ ger

__ __ ny

__ __ sic

__ __ __ ceries

__ __ gle

NOUN ★	VERB ➡	ADJECTIVE 😊	ADVERB ?
bagel	joking	brutal	suddenly
photo	napping	skunky	now
yogurt	kidding	putrid	painfully
yo-yo	sleeping	crazy	completely

Camping Trip Prep

Fremont and Milo had to prepare for their camping trip. "Ugh! What's that

_____ odor?" asked Fremont. "I don't smell anything,"
😊

replied Milo. "Are you _____ ?" Fremont threw a frozen
➡

_____ at him. "That aroma is _____ !"
★   😊

"Oh no!" said Milo, _____ understanding. "Remember
?

that fish I caught?" "The one that looked like a _____ ,
★

and you wanted to preserve it for display?" responded Fremont.

"I wrapped it in my sleeping bag to keep it safe," said Milo.

"And then you forgot." "And then I forgot." "Oops!"

said Fremont, _____ laughing. "I
?

guess I'll be sleeping on the ground," said Milo.

Final Stable Syllables

Some **syllables** are common at the ends of words.
Looking for these syllables can help you chunk and read longer words.

Consonant + le	Other
bat/**tle**	na/**tion**
ca/**ble**	ten/**sion**
un/**cle**	adven/**ture**
shuf/**fle**	pres/**sure**

Add the missing **final syllable**.

ea __ __ __

erup __ __ __ __

puz __ __ __

trea __ __ __

cir __ __ __

pic __ __ __

tur __ __ __

nee __ __ __

NOUN	VERB	ADJECTIVE	ADVERB
★	→	☺	?
tree	giggle	maple	obviously
needle	topple	pickled	quite
elephant	grumble	purple	clearly
steeple	wobble	delectable	surely

Fox and the Grapes

Fox spotted a bunch of _____ grapes high up. "If I were able to
☺

reach those juicy grapes, I could _____ fill my belly," thought
?

Fox. Fox tried to climb the _____ , but it proved too slick. Each
★

time he lunged at the picture-perfect grapes, his paw slipped,

and he would _____ to the ground. With
→

each failed climb, Fox's frustration grew. At last he thought, "I'm

a fool to waste my time. These grapes are _____ sour,
?

not _____ like I want." Fox went off, continuing to
☺

_____ about sour grapes. *Those who can't get*
→

what they want often pretend what they wanted wasn't

worth it after all.

PHONICS AND WORD STUDY

r-Controlled Vowel Syllables

When a vowel is followed by **r**, the letter **r** affects the vowel sound. The vowel and the **r** act as a team and must stay in the same syllable. Knowing this can help you chunk and read longer words.

mar/ket   **per**/fect   **cir**/cus   **for**/tune   **hur**/ry

Add the missing **r-controlled vowel syllable**.

_ _ _ _ ty **40**

_ _ _ _ _ er

_ _ _ _ _ _ day

soc _ _ _ _

_ _ _ tains

doc _ _ _ _

_ _ _ key

mon _ _ _ _

NOUN	VERB	ADJECTIVE	ADVERB
★	➡	😊	?
doctor	harvests	powerful	interestingly
master	hurries	precise	terribly
badger	sends	terrific	rather
brain	shouts	rubbery	very

The Nose Knows

A dog's sense of smell is _____ useful for finding people and things.
?

Scientists have found that a dog's sense of smell is over ten thousand times more

_____ than our own. Why are they such _____
😊   😊

smellers? They have about three hundred million smell receptors on

their nose. A receptor is what _____ the smell signal
➡

to the _____ . Humans have about six million
★

receptors. The other _____ difference is in the dog's
😊

brain. The part of the brain that _____ smells is
➡

forty times larger than ours! This is why people's best friend, the dog, is

the ultimate smell _____ .
★

Vowel Team Syllables

Many vowel sounds are made using **vowel teams**, such as
ai, ay, ea, ee, oa, ow, ou, igh, oo, oi, oy, ey, ie, and **ei**.
These vowel teams must stay in the same syllable.
Knowing this can help you chunk and read longer words.

r**ai**l/r**oa**d   m**ai**n/t**ai**n

Add the missing **vowel team syllable**.

__ __ __ __ box    mon __ __ __

high __ __ __    four __ __ __ __

bal __ __ __ __    rain __ __ __

__ __ __ saw    yel __ __ __

NOUN ★	VERB →	ADJECTIVE ☺	ADVERB ?
entertainment	enjoy	overjoyed	highly
cartoons	view	eager	surely
theater	experience	saddened	barely
showboats	plow	delighted	fairly

Let's See a Show!

Dear Cousin Cookie,

I am so _____ (☺) and _____ (☺) for your visit. I

want to _____ (→) all the amazing sites with you. My mom says you

like _____ (★) . We can get tickets, but I am not sure what kind of

_____ (★) you like? Do you like musicals? There are many that are

_____ (?) acclaimed. Would you like to see a serious play, or maybe

a comedy? We could see a Shakespeare play in the park if that

appeals to you. Let me know as soon as you

can! I am _____ (?)

_____ (☺) to see a show

with you!

Final-e Syllables

Spellings such as **a_e** in **brake** and **i_e** in **slide** stand for long vowel sounds.

These spellings act as a team and must stay in the same syllable. Knowing this can help you chunk and read longer words.

com/p<u>ete</u>   t<u>ime</u>/less

Add the missing **final-e syllable**.

rep __ __ __ __

mis __ __ __ __

ex __ __ __ __ __

__ __ __ __ ty

__ __ __ __ ball

__ __ __ __ walk

xylo __ __ __ __ __

__ __ __ __ book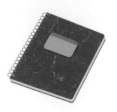

NOUN ★	VERB ➡	ADJECTIVE 😊	ADVERB ?
ocean	eroded	sandy	extremely
shoreline	deflated	icy	generally
island	sank	lonesome	never
prairie	invaded	pricey	barely

Breaker Is a Fix

Ozone Village had a problem. Every fall when the storm season arrived

on the _____ ★ , the beach _____ ➡ . The

_____ ? _____ 😊 beach was pounded by storm waves.

With each crashing wave, the beach became smaller and more _____ 😊 .

Every spring, the village purchased more sand. They needed a solution to blockade

the waves. So, they made a breaker. A breaker is a wall of large rocks that protrudes

into the _____ ★ . The waves collide with the

breaker instead of the beach. This year the village won't

have to devote a lot of money to replace the village

_____ ★ .

Root Words

A **root word** has no prefix or suffix.
It's the most basic part of a word.
Many words share the same root.
Knowing the root can help you read, spell, and define words.

| <u>expect</u> | <u>expect</u>ing | <u>expect</u>ed | un<u>expect</u>ed |

Write the **root** for each group of words.

_____	player	playful	replay
_____	unsigned	signing	signature
_____	unhappy	happily	unhappily
_____	sadness	sadly	saddest

Write four **root words**. Add three examples of words you can make from them.

1. _____ _____ _____ _____

2. _____ _____ _____ _____

3. _____ _____ _____ _____

4. _____ _____ _____ _____

NOUN	VERB	ADJECTIVE	ADVERB
★	→	☺	?
president	build	celebratory	busily
organization	cook	selfless	helplessly
human	paint	humane	actively
robot	organize	secret	humanely

President Carter Builds Houses

Former president Jimmy Carter became the oldest living _____ ★

on October 1, 2019, when he celebrated his ninety-fifth birthday. President Carter

served as the thirty-ninth president of the United States from 1997 to 1981. A few

years after his presidency, President Carter and his wife, Rosalynn, began their

_____ ☺ work with Habitat for Humanity. This volunteer organization

helps people _____ → and _____ → houses for

themselves. President Carter has been _____ ?

building houses with the organization since 1984. He is

even _____ ? building houses now

at ninety-five years old! There is nothing more

_____ ☺ than that!

Using Prefixes and Suffixes to Sound Out Words

A **prefix** is a word part added to the beginning of a word, such as **un** and **re**.

A **suffix** is a word part added to the end of a word, such as **ed** and **ful**.

Quickly seeing these common word parts can help you chunk and read longer words.

<u>un</u>like   hope<u>ful</u>   <u>re</u>discover<u>ed</u>

Circle the **prefix** and/or **suffix(es)** in each word.

unreal	replay	disagreeable
preordered	suddenly	helpless
unprotected	beautifully	reopened
disturbing	mistreated	premeasured

NOUN ★	VERB →	ADJECTIVE ☺	ADVERB ?
wings	dissolved	careless	secretly
kites	colored	wise	cleverly
airplanes	soaked	silly	foolishly
helicopters	absorbed	prudent	frequently

The Myth of Icarus

Daedalus and his son Icarus were held captive on an island. Daedalus had a plan

to escape. He _____ made _____ from feathers and
       ?   ★

wax. Daedalus warned Icarus, "If you fly too low, you will be _____
                                                        →

by the seawater. If you fly too high, you will disappear because the sun will melt

the wax." Icarus was so _____ , and he flew higher
                          ☺

and higher. He _____ did not heed his
                 ?

father's _____ warning. The hot sun
        ☺

_____ the wax. Icarus fell into
    →

the sea. To this day, people remember to not

go too high, nor too low, but maintain a

steady course.

Chunking Big Words to Read Them

When you see a long word while reading, chunk it into smaller parts to read it.

If the word has two consonants in the middle, such as **rubber**, divide the word between the two consonants: **rub/ber**.

<u>**nap/kin**</u>   <u>**mag/net**</u>

Write the two parts of each word.

middle   _____   _____

monster   _____   _____

complex   _____   _____

basket   _____   _____

publish   _____   _____

NOUN ★	VERB →	ADJECTIVE ☺	ADVERB ?
serpent	spotted	horrid	secretly
mountain	napped with	little	festively
monster	ridden	enormous	quietly
pillow	chased	gooey	eventually

Champ the Lake Monster

Vermont is known for its _____ (☺) maple syrup. But its other claim to

fame might be its mystery _____ (★) . Said to live in the 125-mile-long

Lake Champlain, Champ has been a local legend for hundreds of years. Described

as a/an _____ (☺) _____ (★) -like beast by those who

claim to have _____ (→) the monster, the existence of Champ has yet to

be proven. Many tourists visit the area and _____ (?)

take part in Champ parades and celebrations. The state of

Vermont _____ (?) passed a law

in 1982 protecting Champ from any harm.

Vermont—a great place for maple syrup and

lake monsters!

PHONICS AND WORD STUDY

Reading Big Words Strategy

When you see a long word while reading, use these five steps to chunk it into smaller parts to read it.

Step 1: Look for common word parts at the beginning, such as prefixes (**un**, **re**, **dis**, **mis**).

Step 2: Look for common word parts at the end, such as suffixes (**ing**, **ed**, **ful**, **less**).

Step 3: Look at what's left. Use what you know about sounding out words and syllable types to chunk it.

Step 4: Sound out all the word parts slowly. It will be close to the real word.

Step 5: Say the word parts fast. Adjust your pronunciation to say it correctly.

Check the steps you use to figure out these words. Write the meaning of each word.

unexpected

☐ Step 1

☐ Step 2

☐ Step 3

☐ Step 4

☐ Step 5

Meaning: _____

_____

_____

misunderstanding

☐ Step 1

☐ Step 2

☐ Step 3

☐ Step 4

☐ Step 5

Meaning: _____

_____

_____

NOUN	VERB	ADJECTIVE	ADVERB
★	→	☺	?
chair	untied	uncomplicated	instantly
fence	uncovered	unpredictable	thoroughly
pillow	entwined	uncomfortable	perfectly
bathtub	disengaged	ingenious	unabashedly

Balloon Transport

"Unbelievable," they all said. I disagreed. I _____ knew it
                                            ?

would work. My _____ plan was to tie helium balloons to a
                    ☺

light _____ or _____ . I knew that if I
          ★   ★

_____ enough balloons, I would be transported weightlessly into
      →

the sky. The day had finally come. With the one hundredth balloon securely fastened,

I began to rise. I quickly _____ the safety
                                →

cord holding me to earth and rose over the backyard.

"How will you come down?" yelled my family, now

_____ aware of my success.
      ?

"I don't know!" I shouted back. "Uh-oh!"

Inflectional Endings with Spelling Changes

When you add **s**, **es**, **ed**, or **ing** to a word, you sometimes have to change the spelling before adding the ending.

1. Double the final consonant

| step | steps | ste**pp**ed | ste**pp**ing |

2. Drop e

| bake | bakes | bak**ed** | bak**ing** |

3. Change y to i

| fry | fr**i**es | fr**i**ed | frying |

Add **s**, **ed**, and **ing** to each word.

	Add **s** or **es**	Add **ed**	Add **ing**
stop	_____	_____	_____
save	_____	_____	_____
cry	_____	_____	_____
grab	_____	_____	_____
vote	_____	_____	_____
supply	_____	_____	_____

NOUN	VERB	ADJECTIVE	ADVERB
★	→	☺	?
ground	raising	moist	actually
weather	gripping	unsteady	simply
sky	tugging	rowdy	remarkably
wind	pulling	blustery	quite

Go Fly a Kite

When the _____ gets _____ , go fly
            ★   ☺

a kite. If you've never flown a kite, it's _____ enjoyable.
                                              ?

Just follow these simple steps. First, you'll need a diamond-shaped kite.

Hold the kite with one hand, _____ the kite string with
                                     →

the other. Then, hold the kite up where the braces meet at the top. The

_____ wind should lift the kite right up into the air.
       ☺

After that, just tug on the line a little bit. The kite should rise into the sky.

Keep _____ the string until the kite is as high as you like.
           →

It's _____ easy!
    ?

Spelling Multisyllabic Words

When spelling a longer word, it is easier to chunk it into smaller parts, or syllables. Then spell each part, one at a time. Think about other words you know with these same or similar parts.

Break each word into syllables. Write each syllable in the blanks.

pineapple   _____ _____ _____

rereading   _____ _____ _____

independence   _____ _____ _____ _____

unforgivable   _____ _____ _____ _____ _____

Look at each picture. Say the picture name. Write each word part by part (syllable by syllable).

_____ _____ _____

_____ _____ _____

_____ _____ _____

_____ _____ _____

NOUN ★	VERB →	ADJECTIVE ☺	ADVERB ?
pouch	encircling	colossal	unquestionably
bump	surrounding	gigantic	normally
basket	preexisting	impressive	extraordinarily
ring	far-reaching	surprising	unusually

Redwood Fairy Rings

California's _____ redwoods are known for their
☺

_____ height. They also grow in a/an _____
☺ ?

strange way. Redwoods have a _____ of oddly shaped wood that is
★

_____ found at the base of the tree. This collar of wood is known
?

as a burl. If the tree dies, the burl sprouts and takes over the _____
→

root system of the parent tree. This is why you might find a perfect circle of

_____ redwoods growing in the forest. The
☺

trees all sprouted from the burl around the dead tree's trunk.

The circle of trees is referred to as a "fairy ring."

Relative Pronouns

Relative pronouns include **who**, **whose**, **whom**, **which**, and **that**. They start a clause, or group of words in a sentence, that tells more about a noun in the sentence.

Use **whose** to show ownership, or something that belongs to someone.
   Whose car is in the driveway? (Someone owns the car.)

Use **who** if you can replace the word with "he."
   The baker **who** won the contest is my friend. (He is my friend.)

Use **whom** if you can replace the word with "him." Remember: Both end with the letter **m**.
   Whom did you call on the phone? (Did you call him on the phone?)

Use **which** if the clause (group of words) is extra information, and not necessary to understand the basic sentence. Often, you separate these words with commas (,).
   Pizza, **which** is made of dough and cheese, is my favorite food. (Pizza is my favorite food.)

Use **that** if the clause (group of words) is necessary in the sentence.
   The bike **that** I bought yesterday is already scratched.

Add a **pronoun** to finish each sentence.

1. The boy _____ won the contest is in my class.

2. This is the book _____ I read for my report.

3. To _____ should I give this money?

4. _____ backpack is blue and has a superhero on it?

NOUN	VERB	ADJECTIVE	ADVERB
★	➡	☺	?
scarf	stirring	swift	amazingly
forest	growing	ugly	deceitfully
branch	circling	fierce	frighteningly
rain	howling	mean	loudly

Stormy Winds

The wind blows strong and _____ .

☺

That which isn't tied down disappears.

Who can stand the _____ wind?

➡

It's as if those who could, grew wings.

Bits of _____ , leaf, and flying nut

★

Swirl and are _____ , with no concern for whom they cut.

➡

The bang, the crash, the _____ moving debris.

?

Whose lost memory? Whose flung trash? Who will haul away that downed tree?

It will not last the _____ storm.

➡

The clouds, which block the sun, will go. Our tempest blown now back to norm.

Progressive Verb Tense

Verbs have different tenses. Some verbs show action in the past. (I **ate** an apple for lunch.)

Some verbs show action that is happening now. (I **am reading** a book.) Verbs that show action that is, was, or will be happening at some point in time are called **progressive verbs**. The action is ongoing, or in progress. These verbs begin with a form of the words "to be," such as **is**, **am**, **was**, **were**, or **will be**.

> I **am** walking. (is happening)
>
> I **was** walking. (was happening)
>
> I **will be** walking. (will be happening)

Finish each sentence using **is**, **am**, **was**, **were**, or **will be**.

1. She _____ reading a book about whales and sharks.

2. He _____ riding his bike slowly up the mountain earlier today.

3. We _____ going on a field trip to a museum tomorrow.

4. I _____ making a birthday cake for my grandmother.

5. They _____ listening to the concert on their phones yesterday.

NOUN ★	VERB ➡	ADJECTIVE 😊	ADVERB ?
hawks	landing	larger	mysteriously
trucks	sliding	louder	simply
nuts	preying	fiercer	brashly
projectiles	crashing	scarier	amply

Mast Years

Crack! The sound of _____ ★ that are _____ ➡ on

parked cars, sidewalks, or even you! You may have noticed in some years past, there

were tons of acorns that were _____ ? falling from trees. You were

not imagining things. Scientists have discovered there is a two- to five-year cycle

where oak trees _____ ? produce an abundance of _____ 😊

acorns. They call these mast years. This results in more animals, like squirrels and

mice, the following year. That means _____ 😊

raptors, like owls, will be _____ ➡

and feasting on these animals. So, from a

simple acorn grows a whole food chain.

Modal Auxiliaries

You sometimes use **helping verbs**, like **can**, **could**, **may**, **might**, and **must**, when writing. They are used to show a request, to show an ability, or to ask for permission.

can: Shows that a person or object is able to do something. (ability)
He **can run** very fast.

could: Shows a past ability.
She **could run** very fast.

may: Shows that someone or something is allowed to do something. It can also be used to request something.
You **may go** to the movies tomorrow. **May** I **go** to the movies, too?

might: Shows that something is possible or likely to happen.
The hurricane **might hit** our town at midnight.

must: Shows that something is necessary or has to happen.
You **must study** a lot for the test on Friday.

Add a **helping verb** to finish each sentence.

1. He _____ walk better before the accident.

2. You _____ help me clean up the classroom!

3. My mother _____ do more in an hour than anyone I know.

4. I _____ visit my grandparents this weekend.

5. You _____ watch TV after you do the dishes.

NOUN	VERB	ADJECTIVE	ADVERB
★	➡	☺	?
plastic	should	right	cautiously
water	could	optimal	objectively
waste	must	expensive	smartly
aluminum	will	helpful	endlessly

Reduce Waste

A big factor in curbing pollution is the idea of reducing. I think that we must

act _____ [?] when we shop. You _____ [➡] keep in

mind the amount of packaging containing the items you buy. Everyone, if they

can, _____ [➡] make the _____ [☺] choice and buy

items with little or no _____ [★] . You should bring your own

cloth bags when you go to a store. We _____ [➡] end the excess

_____ [★] that our shopping creates.

If everyone can think about buying items

with little or no packaging, we might

_____ [?] make a dent in our

increased waste. We must all do better!

Adjective Order

Adjectives are describing words. When there is more than one adjective before a noun, they are written in a specific order: **opinion**, **size**, **condition**, **age**, **shape**, **color**, **pattern**, **origin**, **material**, **purpose**. Often there is a word like **a**, **an**, or **the** before these other words.

opinion	ugly, pretty, tasty	**color**	green, purple, reddish
size	large, tiny, tall	**pattern**	striped, zigzag, dotted
condition	dirty, wet, rich	**origin**	American, Asian, Spanish
age	old, young, new	**material**	wooden, cotton, plastic
shape	long, thin, square	**purpose**	shopping, riding, sleeping

Put these **adjectives** in order.

1. wooden, beautiful

_____ _____ **table**

2. yellow, old, hungry

_____ _____ _____ **monster**

3. pretty, antique, porcelain, British

_____ _____ _____

_____ **plate**

4. bluish, square, nice, new, striped

_____ _____ _____

_____ _____ **blanket**

NOUN ★	VERB →	ADJECTIVE ☺	ADVERB ?
rancher	pulled	colossal	shockingly
banker	shouted	puny	accidentally
goat	cried	gargantuan	surprisingly
farmer	tugged	meager	suddenly

The Bountiful Beet

One day a _____ (★) , _____ (?) , found an

enormous round red-and-white-striped British sugar beet growing in his garden. He

_____ (→) , but the beet wouldn't budge. His wife and children helped.

They couldn't get the stubborn _____ (☺) gleaming spherical beet to

move. He had an idea. He got the villagers and they _____ (→) . They

each held each other's waists and made a chain. With the whole

village helping, _____ (?) the beet was

released from the ground. That night, the farmer made a

delicious _____ (☺) spicy pink beet soup.

"When everyone works together, everyone gets rewarded,"

said the farmer.

Prepositional Phrases

A **preposition** is a connecting word, such as **about**, **after**, **at**, **before**, **behind**, **by**, **during**, **for**, **from**, **in**, **of**, **over**, **past**, **to**, **under**, **up**, and **with**. A **prepositional phrase** is a group of words in a sentence that begins with a preposition and ends with an object. The prepositional phrase does **not** contain a verb or the subject of the sentence. It gives more information about how, when, why, who, where, or which one.

> We found the kitten **under the sofa**. (where)
>
> I ate the leftover spaghetti **from last night's supper**. (when)

Circle the **prepositional phrase** in each sentence.

1. Mom told us to be quiet during the movie.

2. The cow from our neighbor's farm had brown and white spots.

3. I did my homework after our dinner.

4. Dad and I drove to the store to buy popcorn.

Write a sentence with each **preposition**.

on _____

before _____

above _____

until _____

NOUN	VERB	ADJECTIVE	ADVERB
★	→	☺	?
Clowns	learned	small	sleepily
Children	located	enormous	naively
Scientists	discovered	special	confidently
Grandmothers	read	fantastic	efficiently

Electric Sensor Sharks

_____ have _____ even more about sharks. These
★ →

ocean creatures have a _____ jelly-like substance in their facial
☺

pores. The jelly helps the shark sense _____ changes in electric
☺

charges. These charges are like the snap of static electricity after you pull a wool

sweater up over your _____ head. In the ocean, the shark's prey has
☺

one kind of charge, while the surrounding water has a different charge. The difference

in the electric charge helps a shark _____
?

determine where its prey is, even under the darkest,

stormiest conditions. The shark proves to be an even

deadlier predator than we once imagined.

Frequently Confused Words

Some words look or sound so much alike that they can be confusing. Paying careful attention to the spellings, sounds, and meanings of these words can help you remember them. Follow these steps to learn these words.

Step 1: Read the word. Say the sounds you hear in it.
Step 2: Spell the word out loud.
Step 3: Write the word as you say the letter names.
Step 4: Think about the word's meaning. Use it in a sentence.

Use the steps to practice the words below. Check the box after completing Steps 1 and 2. Write the word for Step 3. Write a sentence for Step 4.

there (place)   Step 1 ☐   Step 2 ☐   Step 3 _____

                       Step 4 _____

they're (they are)   Step 1 ☐   Step 2 ☐   Step 3 _____

                       Step 4 _____

their (possession)   Step 1 ☐   Step 2 ☐   Step 3 _____

                       Step 4 _____

your (possession)   Step 1 ☐   Step 2 ☐   Step 3 _____

                       Step 4 _____

you're (you are)   Step 1 ☐   Step 2 ☐   Step 3 _____

                       Step 4 _____

NOUN ★	VERB →	ADJECTIVE 😊	ADVERB ?
ship	called	pleasant	fantastically
restaurant	invited	horrible	exceptionally
meal	led	delightful	remarkably
table	assigned	unusual	typically

Lunch on a Ship

Dear Cousin Maeve,

When you visit me in Baltimore, you're _____ to a/an
→

_____ lovely lunch on a ship! Don't worry about your seasickness.
?

The _____ doesn't leave the dock. The only waves are from passing
★

Jet Skis. It's _____ _____ on the water. We can
? 😊

get a bucket or two of crabs and a mallet to break them open. They're not

too expensive. It's a Maryland tradition. Maryland is famous for their

_____ crabs. They come from nearby Chesapeake
😊

Bay. The blue crab was even named the state crustacean! If you can

get over your seasickness and aversion to shellfish, we will have

a/an _____ time there!
😊

Capitalization

What begins with a **capital letter**?

- the first word in a sentence
- the word **I**
- the name of a holiday, month, and exact place
- the name and title of a specific person
- the title of a book

We eat turkey and watch football games on **Thanksgiving**.
My family moved to **California** last **September**.
Mrs. Lee, our teacher, read **Charlotte's Web** to us.

Fix each sentence.

1. what does your family do for christmas?

_____

2. did mr. sanchez start his new business in march or april?

_____

3. we are traveling to japan and england this summer.

_____

4. i just finished reading harry potter, and it's long!

_____

5. i hope maria and jackson will visit this easter.

_____

NOUN	VERB	ADJECTIVE	ADVERB
★	➡	😊	?
coast	erupt	giant	finally
seashore	spit out	remarkable	wonderfully
airport	release	volcanic	recently
ocean	explode	tiny	surprisingly

Volcanoes Blowing Bubbles

John Lyons, a scientist with the Alaska Volcano Observatory, has _____
?

discovered that undersea volcanoes can _____ a
➡

_____ bubble of gas. Monitoring the gas bubbles is another clue
😊

as to when a volcano may be about to _____ . His discovery was
➡

published in the October 14, 2019, issue of *Nature Geoscience.* The bubble grows

underwater as the pressure from the _____ magma builds beneath
😊

it. _____ , the volcano erupts and
?

sends gas and hot ash high into the sky. Scientists

observed this activity after the 2017 eruption of the

underwater volcano Bogoslof, part of the Aleutian

Islands off the Alaskan _____ .
★

Commas in Quotations

Use a **comma** to separate a direct quote and who is saying it.
The comma appears **before** the quotation mark (").

"I am not feeling well," said Tomás.

My mother said, "You better watch out!"

Add the missing **comma** in each sentence.

1. "Don't upset me like that " yelled Olivia.

2. "I really want to be included on the team " said Marcos.

3. The hawk swooped down and screeched "Caw! Caw!"

4. Jason said "My favorite animal is the fierce lion."

Write sentences showing what someone might say in a story. Create a conversation between two or more characters.

1. _____

_____

2. _____

_____

3. _____

_____

4. _____

_____

NOUN ★	VERB →	ADJECTIVE ☺	ADVERB ?
moment	replied	curly	loudly
second	snapped	leafy	oddly
day	looked	tall	safely
instance	growled	ancient	suspiciously

Rooster and Fox

Rooster was _____ perched in his _____ tree.
                    ?   ☺

"Terrific news," said Fox. "All the animals have decided to put our differences aside;

we will now live as friends from this _____ forward." Rooster,
                                              ★

distracted, _____ off in the distance. "Come shake my hand, new
                   →

friend," said Fox. "I will, but first, I see Dog on his way," _____
                                                                      →

Rooster. "Dog! I'd better leave," said Fox. "Don't you want to see your

new friend, Dog?" "No, I better not, he may not have heard the

good news," Fox _____ yelled,
                        ?

running away.

A trickster is easily tricked.

Quotes

Use **quotation marks** when quoting the exact words someone says.

"I will be late to the meeting," said Mr. Chin.

The giant screamed, "Fee, fi, fo, fum!"

Add the missing **quotation marks** in each sentence.

1. I would really prefer pizza for my party, said the girl.

2. We can play soccer on Saturday, said Dad.

3. What are you dressing up as for Halloween? asked Sophia.

4. Run! Run! shouted the boy. The monster is behind you!

Write sentences showing a conversation between you and a friend or family member.

1. _____

_____

2. _____

_____

3. _____

_____

4. _____

_____

NOUN	VERB	ADJECTIVE	ADVERB
★	➡	😀	?
words	contains	moving	deeply
speeches	repeats	hopeful	frankly
utterances	echoes	memorable	profoundly
proclamations	highlights	powerful	effectively

America's Orator

Martin Luther King Jr.'s _____ words helped change America. King's
😀

"I Have a Dream" speech was delivered in 1968 on the steps of the Lincoln Memorial

to a crowd of 250,000 civil rights activists. The speech _____
➡

the phrase "I have a dream" several times for effect. King _____
?

touched the nation with these _____ : "I have a dream that my
★

four little children will one day live in a nation where they will not

be judged by the color of their skin but by the content of

their character." He delivered a _____
😀

and _____ appropriate call for
?

justice in America.

Compound Sentences

A **compound sentence** has two sentences put together.
The words **and**, **but**, **or**, and **so** are used to make a compound sentence.
A comma (**,**) is put before one of these words.

> Ben went to the movies**, and** I stayed home to rest.
> I like to sleep late**, but** I have to get up early tomorrow.

Put together the two sentences to make a **compound sentence**.

I love gymnastics. My sister loves soccer.

_____

_____

We like to eat chocolate. Our school doesn't allow it.

_____

_____

We can go to the park. We can go to the mall.

_____

_____

NOUN	VERB	ADJECTIVE	ADVERB
★	→	☺	?
residents	change	unique	adequately
locals	support	unusual	duly
people	elect	unlikely	sufficiently
insects	vote for	uncommon	justly

The District of Columbia

When is a city not in a state? When it's the US capital. The city, known as the District

of Columbia, or DC, is run by Congress, and therefore is not part of any state. Many

issues arise from this _____ city government, and one such issue is
                                    ☺

that the _____ lack representation in Congress. They are not allowed
                    ★

to _____ any senators in Congress. Residents wish
        →

to _____ how the _____
        →   ☺

city is governed, because they feel that they are not

_____ represented, and it is unfair.
        ?

Citizens of our nation's capital feel like they have no

say at the Capitol Building.

Text Structure: Sequence

Writers of informational text use different ways to **structure** their writing. One way is to put the information in **sequence**, or **time order**.

These signal words often alert a reader that the text is organized this way: **first, second, third, next, then, last, after, finally, before, in the beginning, to start, meanwhile, in the middle, at the end**. The writer might also use **dates in order (such as 1776, 1865, and 2020)**.

Fill in the **sequence** paragraph. Write about an interesting topic, like building or making something.

The **first** step in _____

is to _____ .

After that, you must _____

_____

_____ .

Next, you need to _____

_____

_____ .

Finally, you _____

_____ .

NOUN	VERB	ADJECTIVE	ADVERB
★	➡	😀	?
crickets	preheated	rubber	finally
beetles	bought	purple	obviously
prunes	lit	wooden	apparently
tulips	painted	mooing	now

The Special Cake

On Maggie's birthday in June, her friends decided to bake her a special cake—one

she would never forget! José grabbed all the cooking utensils: mixer, pots, pans,

and a _____ spatula. Then, Sonia gathered the ingredients: flour,
                😀

milk, and chocolate, with _____ and _____ to
                              ★   ★

add flavor. After that, Yan mixed the ingredients and _____ the
                                                              ➡

oven. It was _____ time for baking. The friends slid the cake into
                    ?

the oven and waited. Twenty minutes. Forty minutes. A little more. At last the cake

was done. Stef and Roberto decorated the cooled cake.

They added _____ flowers and
                    😀

a _____ puppy on top—Maggie's
        😀

favorite. So, there was only one thing left to do. Eat it!

Text Structure: Cause/Effect

Writers of informational text use different ways to **structure** their writing. One way is to explain the **causes** and **effects** of something. The causes are **why** something happens. The effects are **what** happens.

These signal words often alert a reader that the text is organized this way: **because, cause, effect, therefore, if…then, as a result, due to, reason, since, leads to, as a consequence, consequently**.

Fill in the **cause and effect** paragraph. Write about an interesting topic, like a natural disaster or other science concept.

Because of _____ , _____

_____

_____ has happened.

Therefore, _____

_____

_____ .

This explains why _____

_____

_____

_____ .

NOUN	VERB	ADJECTIVE	ADVERB
★	→	😊	?
home run	creates	ordinary	currently
star	causes	traditional	lately
base	ensures	typical	today
purse	produces	common	now

Home Run Hitter

In baseball, what causes a hit to be a home run or a pop-up easy out? It's all about

the angles. Since 2015, there's been an uptick in home runs. _____ **?** ,

experts are saying the increase is because the batters have changed the way they

swing the bat. The _____ 😊 technique is to hit the top of the ball.

This angle _____ → a strong fly ball, but _____ →

a limited chance of getting the hitter a _____ ★ .

However, today's batters have changed the angle. Now they hit

the bottom third of the ball with a slight lift. This swing is

the cause of the record home runs major league teams are

_____ **?** experiencing.

Text Structure: Problem/Solution

Writers of informational text use different ways to **structure** their writing. One way is to **identify a problem** and **detail the solution** or solutions.

These signal words often alert a reader that the text is organized this way: **problem**, **solution**, **solve**, **as a result**, **consequently**, **since**, **therefore**, **because of**, **leads to**, **due to**, **as**, **then**.

Fill in the **problem and solution** paragraph. Write about an interesting topic, like an environmental issue.

The **problem** was _____

_____

_____ .

This problem happened **because** _____

_____

_____

_____ .

The problem was finally **solved** when _____

_____

_____

_____ .

NOUN	VERB	ADJECTIVE	ADVERB
★	➡	😊	?
pollutants	controlling	fantastic	sadly
chemicals	reducing	ultimate	unfortunately
irritants	decreasing	urban	noticeably
poisons	lessening	natural	tragically

Plant a Tree

One of the easiest things that people can do to help the environment is plant a

tree. Trees could be called the _____ problem solvers. Increases

(😊)

in gases that _____ warm the atmosphere are a problem, but

(?)

trees soak in those _____ and clean the air. If your home is

(★)

_____ warm, you can cool it off by planting trees. Their shade is

(?)

like a/an _____ air conditioner. Are you losing too

(😊)

much topsoil, or are your lands flooding? Trees can

solve that problem, too. A tree's roots hold

the soil in place and soak up rainwater,

_____ flooding. Plant a

(➡)

tree, and save the environment!

Similes and Metaphors

Similes and **metaphors** are used by writers to compare things.
Similes use the words **like** or **as** to compare things.

> My cat is **like** a little tiger.
>
> That kitten is **as** cute **as** a button.

Metaphors directly compare things.

> Dr. Chang **is** an angel.
>
> Larry **is** a big chicken.

Finish each sentence using a **simile** or **metaphor**.

1. This winter is like _____

_____ .

2. My sister is as _____ as a

_____ .

3. Our old car is like _____

_____ .

4. The world is _____

_____ .

5. Laughter is _____

_____ .

NOUN ★	VERB →	ADJECTIVE 😊	ADVERB ?
warriors	racing	raucous	endlessly
soldiers	storming	wide	tirelessly
athletes	flowing	large	wildly
competitors	thundering	serious	bravely

Marathon Day

Tens of thousands of runners make up a _____ river of

[😊]

_____ . Their legs _____ lift and fall like

[★]   [?]

ripples in the water. Tens of thousands of runners, as fast as rockets, on the move.

Rushing, _____ , pounding their feet up and down the city. A

[→]

stampeding herd. Twenty-six miles. They wind their way like a river of pounding

hearts. Tens of thousands of runners, tens of thousands of _____ .

[★]

Shouting, cheering, _____ fans and _____

[😊]   [→]

choppers filming overhead. They surge through the streets like a jolt of electric current.

Charging each borough along the way. Marathon Day!

Idioms

An **idiom** is a group of words that has a meaning specific to a language. This meaning is different from the actual words. For example, if a writer says, "It's raining cats and dogs," it means that it is "raining hard"—not that cats and dogs are falling from the sky.

Match the **idiom** to its meaning.

Idiom	**Meaning**
At the drop of a hat	A great idea or plan
The ball is in your court	It is up to you to take the next step or to do something
Barking up the wrong tree	Right away; instantly
Best thing since sliced bread	You are teasing me
You're pulling my leg	It is very expensive
Costs an arm and a leg	Looking in the wrong place or accusing the wrong person of something
Feel a bit under the weather	You're exactly right
Hit the nail on the head	Someone is sick

NOUN	VERB	ADJECTIVE	ADVERB
★	→	☺	?
horses	crammed	mighty	deftly
tigers	spotted	hairy	oddly
rattlesnakes	scrambled	strong	happily
worms	yanked	outrageous	strangely

Sally Ann and Davy Crockett

Like all tales starring Sally Ann Thunder Ann Whirlwind, this one's a doozy. You

might even think I'm pulling your leg, but hold on. Sally Ann was a wild woman of the

Wild West. She was as _____ as a bear and as _____
(☺)   (☺)

as a tornado. One day, Sally Ann saw something strange. A raccoon was sitting

_____ in a tree. Except the raccoon wasn't sitting in a tree. He
?

was sitting on top of Davy Crockett's head. "Help!" Davy

shouted. Just then, Sally Ann _____
→

a half dozen _____ and
★

_____ . Cool as a cucumber, she
★

tied them into a lasso and swung it to free Davy.

Sally Ann saved the day. A piece of cake!

WRITING: Spelling, Grammar, and Story Structure

Characters and Settings

The **characters** are whom the story is about. We learn about characters from what they say, think, and do. We also learn about them from what other characters say about them.

The **setting** is where and when a story takes place.

Fill in the chart using information from your favorite stories.

Story:
Setting:
Main Character:
What You Know About the Character and How:

Story:
Setting:
Main Character:
What You Know About the Character and How:

NOUN ★	VERB →	ADJECTIVE 😀	ADVERB ?
peanut	gobbled	scary	miraculously
pickle	slurped	giant	suddenly
puppet	swallowed	monstrous	promptly
porcupine	drank	deadly	accidently

Pinocchio and the Whale

Pinocchio was a _____ ★ . One day, his friend Geppetto had an

accident and fell into the cold, dark sea, where a whale _____ ?

_____ → him. Pinocchio knew he must save Geppetto. Pinocchio

summoned his courage and dove deep into the bleak black sea, past shipwrecks and

_____ 😀 clams, schools of stingrays, and swirling octopuses. He found

the whale and bravely jumped into its belly. "I knew you'd find me!" said Geppetto.

They built a fire, causing the whale to sneeze. Geppetto

and Pinocchio were free. Pinocchio proved

to be so _____ 😀 that

he _____ ? became

a real boy.

Point of View

Point of view is how a story is told. It affects the information the reader gets from the story's narrator—the person telling the story.

First Person Point of View: The narrator, or person telling the story, is **in** the story. Key words used are **I** and **my**. We "hear" and "see" the story through the narrator's eyes only. Therefore, the information the narrator can provide is limited.

Second Person Point of View: The narrator is speaking directly to the reader, using words like **you** or **your**. Few stories are told in this way.

Third Person Point of View: The narrator, or person telling the story, is **not in** the story. We "hear" and "see" the story from an outside voice.

Fill in the chart using information from your favorite stories.

Story:	
Point of View:	**How You Know:**

Story:	
Point of View:	**How You Know:**

NOUN ★	VERB →	ADJECTIVE 😀	ADVERB ?
hut	exclaimed	crunchy	savagely
cave	cried	savory	surely
door	shrieked	delicious	fiercely
castle	shouted	quick	confidently

The Bear, the Wolf, the Pigs

"Oh no!" I thought. "Bear will _____ catch me!" I was so
?

worried about becoming Bear's _____ meal, I hadn't realized I
😀

was suddenly lost. I spotted a _____ and raced for it. I banged
★

_____ on the door. "Let me in, please!" I _____ .
?   →

Papa Pig peeked out but then slammed the curtains closed. I heard frightened voices

inside. "It's Wuh…Wuh…Wolf!" squealed Papa Pig. "Don't

let him in," cautioned Mama Pig. "Let me in!" I pleaded.

"We must join forces to prevent Bear from eating us!"

"Bear!" _____ the Pigs. "You alone
→

will surely satisfy his hunger. Good luck, our dear old

enemy. Good luck!"

Prefixes

A **prefix** is a word part added to the beginning of a word. It changes the meaning of the word.

un, **dis** = not or the opposite of

re = again

mis = bad, wrong, incorrectly

happy	**un**happy	(not happy)
like	**dis**like	(the opposite of like)
read	**re**read	(read again)
treat	**mis**treat	(treat badly or wrongly)

Add **un**, **dis**, **re**, or **mis** to finish each word.

_____appear   _____friendly

_____obey   _____able

_____understood   _____make

_____clear   _____play

_____approve   _____place

NOUN ★	VERB ➡	ADJECTIVE 😃	ADVERB ?
observer	flapping	massive	especially
scientist	floating	billowy	uniquely
child	fluttering	amazing	slightly
enthusiast	whizzing	unbelievable	shockingly

Monarch Migration

Every year, the _____ **?** beautiful monarch butterfly

migrates from its home in North America to the mountains in central

Mexico. It's amazing to see the orange-and-black butterflies converge

in _____ 😃 clouds of wings _____ ➡ by.

Experts don't disagree. They say the best time to see the migration is when

the butterflies begin their return trip to North America. This offers

a/an _____ ★ an unmistakable chance to see millions

of butterflies _____ ➡ on the trees, seemingly turning

them orange. If you ever want to see this _____ 😃

sight, head down to Mexico during the month of

February. You won't be disappointed!

Prefixes

A **prefix** is a word part added to the beginning of a word.
It changes the meaning of the word.

pre = before

sub = under or below

mid = halfway or middle point

super = above, beyond

ir = not

read	**pre**read	(read before)
way	**sub**way	(pathway under the surface)
day	**mid**day	(middle of the day)
human	**super**human	(beyond human)
regular	**ir**regular	(not regular)

Add **pre**, **sub**, **mid**, **super**, or **ir** to finish each word.

_____cook   _____game

_____natural   _____write

_____responsible   _____freezing

_____plan   _____star

_____way   _____replaceable

NOUN	VERB	ADJECTIVE	ADVERB
★	➡	☺	?
compass	presumed	faulty	quickly
mirror	believed	unreliable	irregularly
auto	observed	superficial	supernaturally
scientist	theorized	tricky	widely

Shifting Poles

Earth's magnetic north is _____ ➡ to be a constant direction. The

big news is that magnetic north is rapidly on the move. Early in 2019, scientists

_____ ➡ magnetic north was shifting _____ ? over the

Northern Hemisphere. In fact, magnetic north is shifting thirty miles a year. Instead

of the North Pole being in the center of the Arctic Circle, it has _____ ?

moved toward Siberia. This makes navigating with a magnetic _____ ★

very _____ ☺ if you are close to

the Arctic Circle. So, if you find yourself

there, or even midway, replace your

compass with your GPS!

Suffixes

A **suffix** is a word part added to the end of a word.
It changes the meaning of the word.
Sometimes the spelling of the base word changes when the suffix
is added.

ful = full of, with

less = without, not

y, **ous** = full of

care	care**ful**	(full of care)
fear	fear**less**	(without fear)
rain	rain**y**	(full of rain)
poison	poison**ous**	(full of poison)

Add **ful**, **less**, **y**, or **ous** to finish each word.

storm_____   weight_____

doubt_____   grass_____

humor_____   hope_____

health_____   odor_____

use_____   need_____

NOUN	VERB	ADJECTIVE	ADVERB
★	➡	😊	?
Hippo	scampered	Bashful	gleefully
Horse	toiled	Enormous	hopefully
Mouse	tugged	Rowdy	rapidly
Unicorn	dashed	Tricky	fearlessly

Rabbit's Field

_____ Rabbit needed to plant his field, but his deceitfulness
          😊

overcame him. He tied a rope to a plow in his field. Soon _____
                                                                    😊

Elephant came along. "I can beat you in a tug-of-war," Rabbit said and smirked.

"Impossible!" replied Elephant, _____ taking hold of the rope.
                                          ?

Rabbit _____ breathlessly across his field. Soon, Haughty
                ➡

_____ came along. "I can beat you in a tug-of-war, too," Rabbit
        ★

boastfully shouted. "No way!" he said, confidently taking the rope. The two

challengers _____ away and pulled hard. With each tug, another
                    ➡

row of Rabbit's field was plowed. The two

_____ tugged all day
        ?

as lazy Rabbit watched and laughed.

Suffixes

A **suffix** is a word part added to the end of a word.
It changes the meaning of the word.
Sometimes the spelling of the base word changes when the suffix
is added.

ment, **tion/ion** = state of being (forms a noun)

ly = in a certain way

ness = quality or state of

amaze	amaze**ment**	(state of being amazed)
correct	correc**tion**	(state of being correct)
slow	slow**ly**	(in a slow way)
happy	happi**ness**	(state of being happy)

Add **ment**, **tion/ion**, **ly**, or **ness** to finish each word.

eager_____   embarrass_____

dark_____   rare_____

equip_____   act_____

achieve_____   friend_____

predict_____   ill_____

NOUN ★	VERB ➡	ADJECTIVE 😊	ADVERB ?
station	walking	special	finally
bathroom	swimming	weightless	surprisingly
capsule	dancing	identical	proudly
shipwreck	relaxing	exact	happily

Splash Before Space

NASA _____ **?** had a celebration for the first all-women space walk. A space walk is when astronauts leave

the space _____ **★** to repair equipment. The astronauts don't train in space, but rather in a giant

_____ **➡** pool! When astronauts slip into NASA's

forty-foot-deep pool, they are _____ **➡** in the

_____ 😊 environment of space. The trainees wear their space suit to

get accustomed to it. While there, they train on a/an _____ 😊 replica

of the space station. There they can _____ **?** practice with the tools

they will use in space. The underwater experience is the closest they can get on Earth

to the weightlessness of space.

Latin Roots

Some **roots**, such as **port**, **scrib/script**, and **spect**, come from Latin. That's a language that was spoken long ago.

You can use the root to figure out the meaning of the word.

Root	Meaning
port	carry
scrib/**script**	write
spect	see/look

Put together the parts of each word and write them below.

ex + port = _____

scrib + ble = _____

spect + a + tor = _____

im + port = _____

pre + script + ion = _____

in + spect = _____

Write a definition for three of the words above, using the **root** as a clue.

Word	Definition
_____	_____
_____	_____
_____	_____

NOUN	VERB	ADJECTIVE	ADVERB
★	➡	😀	?
eggs	devour	furry	scarily
snakes	tickle	rotten	crazily
puppies	juggle	spotted	lazily
babies	sniff	smelly	happily

The Coliseum

On the edge of town stands the Coliseum—a large building shaped like two

_____ . People and their _____
          ★   😀

_____ gather to watch the latest entertainment events. The
          ★

Coliseum owners have imported acts from all over the world for this week's show.

There are lions that _____ _____ rabbits, and
                              ➡   😀

acrobats that _____ _____ clowns and twirl from
                      ?   ➡

ropes tied to the ceiling. As a newspaper employee, I was assigned to report on

this important and spectacular event. But all I wanted to do was be a spectator.

So, I quickly scribbled some notes after the first act, then sat

back and _____ enjoyed!
                  ?

Latin Roots

Some **roots**, such as **struct**, **ven/vent**, and **vid/vis**, come from Latin.
That's a language that was spoken long ago.
You can use the root to figure out the meaning of the word.

Root	Meaning
<u>struct</u>	build
<u>ven</u>/<u>vent</u>	come
<u>vid</u>/<u>vis</u>	see

Put together the parts of each word and write them below.

con + struct + ion = _____

con + vene = _____

vis + u + al + ize = _____

de + struct + ion = _____

con + ven + tion = _____

in + vis + ible = _____

Write a definition for three of the words above, using the **root**
as a clue.

Word	Definition
_____	_____
_____	_____
_____	_____

NOUN	VERB	ADJECTIVE	ADVERB
★	→	😊	?
earthquake	bring in	horrible	quickly
hurricane	raise	terrible	instantly
tornado	generate	catastrophic	unfortunately
tsunami	save	crushing	shockingly

Indestructible

Our new mayor has decided to construct a new convention center in

town. He says it will attract visitors from all over the country and

_____ tons of money. The construction workers
            →

labored for months. The building _____ grew
                                            ?

taller and taller until it was visible from the neighboring town. On

the opening day, the mayor convened all the town's residents. But one

hour before the ribbon-cutting ceremony, a _____
                                                    😊

_____ _____ hit. The destruction of
        ★   ?

the building was _____ . But we aren't a town of
                        😊

quitters. We will rebuild, bigger and better. Our determination is

visible. We are indestructible!

Greek Roots

Some **roots**, such as **bio**, **graph**, **phon**, **auto**, **tri**, and **oct**, come from Greek. That's a language that was spoken long ago. It's still spoken today. You can use the root to figure out the meaning of the word.

Root	Meaning
<u>bio</u>	life
<u>graph</u>	write
<u>phon</u>	sound/hear
<u>auto</u>	self
<u>tri</u>	three
<u>oct</u>	eight

Put together the parts of each word and write them below.

bio + graph + y = _____

micro + phone = _____

oct + opus = _____

auto + graph = _____

tri + angle = _____

Write a definition for three of the words above, using the **root** as a clue.

Word	Definition
_____	_____
_____	_____
_____	_____

NOUN	VERB	ADJECTIVE	ADVERB
★	➡	😀	?
computer	laugh	interesting	Recently
phonograph	giggle	remarkable	Yesterday
bionic arm	chuckle	fascinating	Today
radio	snort	special	Last week

Grandfather

_____ , I wrote a biography of the most
        ?

_____ person I know—my grandfather. I
      😀

called him on the telephone to interview him. I knew he

had eight kids (including our town's only set of triplets),

but I didn't know people nicknamed him Mr. Octopus

because of that! How _____ ! It made
          😀

me _____ . My grandfather recalled his
     ➡

first automobile and seeing other inventions for the first time—

like the television, _____ , and _____ . He even
       ★   ★

remembered seeing the first astronauts travel into space. Someday I will write my

autobiography, and I hope I have _____ facts like these to include.
          😀

Greek Roots

Some **roots**, such as **geo**, **scope**, **tele**, **photo**, **astro**, and **therm**, come from Greek. That's a language that was spoken long ago. It's still spoken today. You can use the root to figure out the meaning of the word.

Root	Meaning
geo	earth
scope	see/look/examine
tele	far/distant
photo	light
astro	star
therm	heat

Put together the parts of each word and write them below.

geo + logy = _____

tele + scope = _____

astro + logy = _____

therm + o + meter = _____

photo + synthesis = _____

Write a definition for three of the words above, using the **root** as a clue.

Word	Definition
_____	_____
_____	_____
_____	_____

NOUN	VERB	ADJECTIVE	ADVERB
★	→	😀	?
laboratory	study	magnificent	really
apartment	investigate	fascinating	obviously
basement	explore	interesting	certainly
barn	observe	unusual	absolutely

We Are Scientists

My best friend and I both want to be scientists when we finish college. I want

to be a geologist. I will _____ (→) Earth's surface, including its

_____ (😀) rocks. I will take photos of everything I find and study

rock samples in my _____ (★) . My best friend wants to be an

astronomer. He will _____ (→) the planets, moons, and stars in our

_____ (😀) solar system. Some of the planets and moons are made of

rock, so we have that in common. He will take photographs of

these sky objects using a powerful telescope he will keep

in his _____ (★) . We _____ (?)

can't wait to become scientists!

Words from Mythology

Some words are based on **myths**. These words are often related to the names of mythical gods or creatures. For example, Atlas was a god who had to carry the sky on his shoulders. He is often seen holding Earth. An atlas is a book of maps, showing places on Earth.

Match the word and the **myth** from which it came. Think about the meaning of each word and how it relates to the myth.

Word	Myth
cereal	**Echo**, who could only repeat what others said
cloth	**Typhon**, the storm giant and father of all monsters
echo	**The Muses**, goddesses of art and science
fortune	**Ceres**, the goddess of agriculture
music	**Vulcan**, god of fire
panic	**Fortuna**, goddess of luck
typhoon	**Clotho**, spun the thread of life
volcano	**Pan**, god of the wild whose look scared people

NOUN ★	VERB →	ADJECTIVE 😊	ADVERB ?
cereal	swept	scary	finally
oatmeal	raced	violent	ultimately
dog food	moved	terrifying	thankfully
spaghetti	raged	petrifying	definitely

Our Violent Earth

This morning, I grabbed a bowl of _____ ★ and plopped in front of the

TV. On my favorite channel was a show about Earth's most _____ 😊

days. The _____ 😊 music blared as hurricanes, typhoons, and

tornadoes _____ → across the land and sea. Volcanoes erupted

bright streams of lava as people in neighboring villages ran in panic. Their screams

echoed through my living room until the chaos

_____ ?

ended. And when it was

_____ ?

over, I was in awe at the

power of Mother Nature.

Shades of Meaning: Adjectives

Adjectives are describing words. Some adjectives mean almost the same thing. However, each adjective has a slightly different meaning.

large   (big)
giant   (very big)
enormous   (very, very big)

Add an **adjective** to finish each sentence: **angry**, **furious**, **happy**, **ecstatic**.

1. We were _____ when we won the gold medal after years of trying.

2. He was _____ that the most important game of the year was canceled.

3. She was _____ that she had a hole in her sock.

4. I was _____ to play at the beach all day.

Write a sentence with each word: **good**, **wonderful**, **phenomenal**.

1. _____

   _____

2. _____

   _____

3. _____

   _____

NOUN ★	VERB ➡	ADJECTIVE 😀	ADVERB ?
rivers	scraping	big	hurriedly
islands	stopping	giant	briskly
ice cubes	scratching	enormous	quickly
mountains	cutting	gargantuan	rapidly

On the Move

The saying that describes moving gradually as "at a glacial pace" has a new, improved

meaning. Glaciers are a very sluggish-moving mass of ice. Like _____ ,
😀

frozen _____ , they move along the surface _____
★   ➡

and eroding the land beneath them. Typically, these _____ glaciers
😀

move only a few inches a day. A glacier in Russia has _____ increased
?

its momentum. In 2013, the Vavilov Ice Cap, found in Siberia, Russia, went from

_____ sixty feet a year to sixty feet a day!
➡

Scientists are not sure what changed the acceleration

but think these glaciers may react to a warming

climate more _____ than
?

was once thought.

Shades of Meaning: Verbs

Verbs are action words. Some verbs mean almost the same thing. However, each verb has a slightly different meaning.

nibbled   (ate by taking little bites)
ate   (ate normally)
devoured   (ate quickly)

Add a **verb** to finish each sentence: **fell, collapsed, strolled, trudged.**

1. He _____ after running in the scorching heat.

2. We _____ along the beach one evening.

3. She tripped and _____ on the sidewalk.

4. He _____ to the principal's office to get his punishment.

Write a sentence with each word: **look, peek, gaze.**

1. _____

_____

2. _____

_____

3. _____

_____

NOUN	VERB	ADJECTIVE	ADVERB
★	➡	😊	?
tree	grow	sweet	very
apple	cultivate	popular	incredibly
kind	farm	bitter	certainly
variety	plant	delicious	wonderfully

An Apple a Day

The apple is a/an _____ _____ fruit. In the US,
                        ?   😊

thousands of varieties of apples are grown, with the Red Delicious being the one

most devoured. Many states _____ apples,
                                  ➡

but Washington farms the most. The apple is even the

state's official fruit. Americans love munching their

apples, ingesting on average nearly fifty pounds of

apples a year! For all of Americans' love of apples, the

only _____ native to the country is the
            ★

crab apple. These are small _____ apples that grow in the wild.
                                   😊

One more _____ interesting fact: Americans imported apples from
                ?

Britain, the first having been planted by Pilgrims.

Synonyms

Synonyms are words that have the same or a similar meaning, such as **big** and **large**. Authors use synonyms in their writing to make their writing more interesting. They can also use synonyms to help readers understand new words.

Match each word to its **synonym**.

Word		Synonym
little		beautiful
smart		miniature
pretty		intelligent
hungry		ancient
old		starving

Write at least one **synonym** for each word.

1. difficult _____   4. slim _____

2. distant _____   5. wealthy _____

3. angry _____   6. exhausted _____

NOUN	VERB	ADJECTIVE	ADVERB
★	➡	☺	?
trap	cornered	silly	really
pit	captured	hilarious	obviously
snare	trapped	laughable	surely
hole	caught	comical	truly

Mouse and Lion

Lion _____ ➡ Mouse. "Wait! Don't eat me! I'm

barely a snack! Someday, I may save your life!" Lion laughed.

"You? Save my life? That's _____ ☺ !

You _____ ? are just a snack. You

can go!" Mouse scampered away saying, "I won't

forget this, Lion!" Not too long after, Lion stepped

into a giant _____ ★ . A net fell. He was

_____ ➡ ! "Pssst, Lion, it's Mouse. I'll chew

through the net and save you!" Mouse chewed on the net, and

soon Lion was able to burst free. "You were right, Mouse! You saved my life!

I _____ ? promise to never eat another mouse!"

Antonyms

Antonyms are words that have the opposite meaning, such as **big** and **small**. Authors use antonyms in their writing to make their writing more interesting.

Match each word to its **antonym**.

Word	**Antonym**
tiny	young
pretty	easy
ancient	huge
difficult	unattractive
furious	thrilled

Write at least one **antonym** for each word.

1. energetic _____   4. quiet _____

2. rich _____   5. strong _____

3. distant _____   6. hardworking _____

NOUN	VERB	ADJECTIVE	ADVERB
★	→	☺	?
Oil	create	large	ultimately
Butter	generate	common	really
Meat	produce	important	unfortunately
Candy	make	necessary	sadly

Harvest the Wind

Wind power is on the rise across America. Iowa excels in harvesting wind energy. Iowa

windfarms _____ over 35 percent of the state's energy. Iowa leads the
→

country in generating renewable wind energy. Renewable energy is a resource that does

not get used up. Wind and solar are two _____ renewable energies.
☺

Nonrenewable energies get used and will, _____ ,
?

not get replenished. _____ and coal are two
★

examples of nonrenewable sources of energy. Iowa is now

one of nearly twenty states that _____
→

_____ quantities of wind energy. As a
☺

renewable energy, wind turbines have _____
?

become a force of nature!

Context Clues

Authors sometimes give clues to help a reader figure out the meaning of a new word. We call these **context clues**. There are many types of context clues. Here are a few:

Definition or Restatement: a definition of the word is given right after it, often in parentheses or followed by **is** or **means**

Synonym: a word with a similar meaning is given, often using the words **or**, **that is**, or **which is**

Example: lists of related things are given, and the word is often followed by **such as**, **include**, **these**, or **for example**

Word Part Clue: the reader can use prefixes, suffixes, and roots to figure out the meaning of the word

Read the sentence, focusing on the **boldfaced** word. Write the type of **context clue** given to help figure out its meaning.

1. _____ The **miniature**, or really small, insect could barely be seen.

2. _____ The car accelerated at a fast rate. **Accelerate** means to speed up.

Write a sentence for one of these words: **observe**, **demolish**, **ginormous**, **evolve**. Provide a context clue to help your reader.

_____

_____

NOUN	VERB	ADJECTIVE	ADVERB
★	➡	☺	?
outdoors	unearth	thrilling	specifically
world	explore	wonderful	suspiciously
environment	detect	exciting	secretly
future	specify	fantastic	curiously

Modern-Day Treasure Hunt

Geocaching is like a treasure hunt, but the map is the Global Positioning System

(GPS). There are websites with geocache locations, or places. There are about ninety

thousand caches in North America! They are given in coordinates, or directions, that

_____ the longitude and latitude degrees on the globe. Once you go
➡

_____ to that place, you need to search for a box, or cache. When
?

you find it, it can be quite _____ ! _____ , you
☺ ?

sign a register, or log, on the computer and take and leave a/an

_____ token, or item. Start geocaching and
☺

_____ the _____ !
➡ ★

ANSWER KEY

6

🔵 PHONICS AND WORD STUDY

Closed Syllables

A **closed syllable** ends in a consonant and has a short vowel sound.
Knowing this can help you chunk and read longer words.

mid/dle   **ab**/sent

Add the missing **closed syllable**.

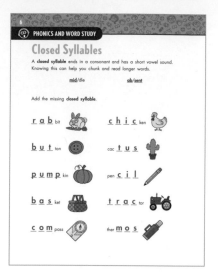

r a b bit   c h i c ken

b u t ton   cac t u s

p u m p kin   pen c i l

b a s ket   t r a c tor

c o m pass   ther m o s

8

🔵 PHONICS AND WORD STUDY

Open Syllables

An **open syllable** ends in a vowel and has a long vowel sound.
Knowing this can help you chunk and read longer words.

ze/bra   si/lent

Add the missing **open syllable**.

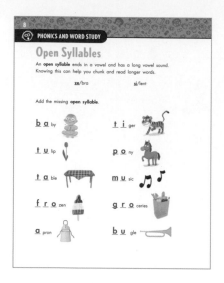

b a by   t i ger

t u lip   p o ny

t a ble   m u sic

f r o zen   g r o ceries

a pron   b u gle

10

🔵 PHONICS AND WORD STUDY

Final Stable Syllables

Some **syllables** are common at the ends of words.
Looking for these syllables can help you chunk and read longer words.

Consonant + le	Other
bat/**tle**	na/**tion**
ca/**ble**	ten/**sion**
un/**dle**	adven/**ture**
shuf/**fle**	pres/**sure**

Add the missing **final syllable**.

ea g l e   erup t i o n

puz z l e   trea s u r e

cir c l e   pic t u r e

tur t l e   nee d l e

12

🔵 PHONICS AND WORD STUDY

r-Controlled Vowel Syllables

When a vowel is followed by **r**, the letter **r** affects the vowel sound.
The vowel and the **r** act as a team and must stay in the same syllable.
Knowing this can help you chunk and read longer words.

mar/ket   **per**/fect   **cir**/cus   **for**/tune   **hur**/ry

Add the missing **r-controlled vowel syllable**.

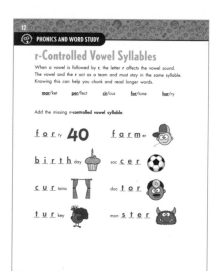

f o r ty **40**   f a r m er

b i r t h day   soc c e r

c u r tains   doc t o r

t u r key   mon s t e r

14

🔵 PHONICS AND WORD STUDY

Vowel Team Syllables

Many vowel sounds are made using **vowel teams**, such as
ai, ay, ea, ee, oa, ow, ou, igh, oo, oi, ay, ey, ie, and **ei**.
These vowel teams must stay in the same syllable.
Knowing this can help you chunk and read longer words.

rail/road   main/tain

Add the missing **vowel team syllable**.

m a i l box   mon k e y

high w a y   four t e e n

bal l o o n   rain b o w

s e e saw   yel l o w

16

🔵 PHONICS AND WORD STUDY

Final-e Syllables

Spellings such as **a_e** in **brake** and **i_e** in **slide** stand
for long vowel sounds.
These spellings act as a team and must stay in the same syllable.
Knowing this can help you chunk and read longer words.

com/**pete**   time/less

Add the missing **final-e syllable**.

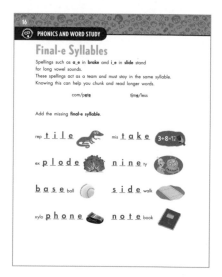

rep t i l e   mis t a k e 3+8=11

ex p l o d e   n i n e ty

b a s e ball   s i d e walk

xylo p h o n e   n o t e book

18

🔵 PHONICS AND WORD STUDY

Root Words

A **root word** has no prefix or suffix.
It's the most basic part of a word.
Many words share the same root.
Knowing the root can help you read, spell, and define words.

expect   **expect**ing   **expect**ed   un**expect**ed

Write the **root** for each group of words.

<u>play</u>   player   playful   replay
<u>sign</u>   unsigned   signing   signature
<u>happy</u>   unhappy   happily   unhappily
<u>sad</u>   sadness   sadly   saddest

Write four **root words**. Add three examples of words you can make from them.

1. <u>Answers will vary</u> _____
2. _____ _____ _____
3. _____ _____ _____
4. _____ _____ _____

20

🔵 PHONICS AND WORD STUDY

Using Prefixes and Suffixes to Sound Out Words

A **prefix** is a word part added to the beginning of a word,
such as **un** and **re**.
A **suffix** is a word part added to the end of a word,
such as **ed** and **ful**.
Quickly seeing these common word parts can help you
chunk and read longer words.

unlike   hope**ful**   **re**discover**ed**

Circle the **prefix** and/or **suffix(es)** in each word.

(un)real   (re)play   (dis)agree(able)
(pre)order(ed)   sudden(ly)   help(less)
(un)protect(ed)   beauti(ful)(ly)   (re)open(ed)
disturb(ing)   (mis)treat(ed)   (pre)measure(d)

22

🔵 PHONICS AND WORD STUDY

Chunking Big Words to Read Them

When you see a long word while reading, chunk it into smaller
parts to read it.
If the word has two consonants in the middle, such as **rubber**,
divide the word between the two consonants: **rub/ber**.

nap/kin   mag/net

Write the two parts of each word.

middle   <u>mid</u>   <u>dle</u>
monster   <u>mon</u>   <u>ster</u>
complex   <u>com</u>   <u>plex</u>
basket   <u>bas</u>   <u>ket</u>
publish   <u>pub</u>   <u>lish</u>

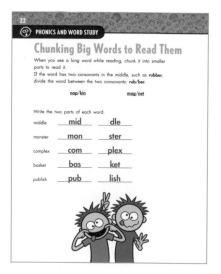

93

---

24 PHONICS AND WORD STUDY

Reading Big Words Strategy

When you see a long word while reading, use these five steps to chunk it into smaller parts to read it.

Step 1: Look for common word parts at the beginning, such as prefixes (un, re, dis, mis).

Step 2: Look for common word parts at the end, such as suffixes (ing, ed, ful, less).

Step 3: Look at what's left. Use what you know about sounding out words and syllable types to chunk it.

Step 4: Sound out all the word parts slowly. It will be close to the real word.

Step 5: Say the word parts fast. Adjust your pronunciation to say it correctly.

Check the steps you use to figure out these words. Write the meaning of each word.

unexpected
- ☑ Step 1
- ☑ Step 2
- ☑ Step 3
- ☑ Step 4
- ☑ Step 5

Meaning: **not expected**

misunderstanding
- ☑ Step 1
- ☑ Step 2
- ☑ Step 3
- ☑ Step 4
- ☑ Step 5

Meaning: **incorrect understanding**

---

26 WRITING: Spelling, Grammar, and Story Structure

Inflectional Endings with Spelling Changes

When you add s, es, ed, or ing to a word, you sometimes have to change the spelling before adding the ending.

1. Double the final consonant
   step   steps   stepp**ed**   stepp**ing**

2. Drop e
   bake   bakes   bak**ed**   bak**ing**

3. Change y to i
   fry   fr**ies**   fr**ied**   frying

Add s, ed, and ing to each word.

	Add s or es	Add ed	Add ing
stop	stops	stopped	stopping
save	saves	saved	saving
cry	cries	cried	crying
grab	grabs	grabbed	grabbing
vote	votes	voted	voting
supply	supplies	supplied	supplying

---

28 WRITING: Spelling, Grammar, and Story Structure

Spelling Multisyllabic Words

When spelling a longer word, it is easier to chunk it into smaller parts, or syllables. Then spell each part, one at a time. Think about other words you know with these same or similar parts.

Break each word into syllables. Write each syllable in the blanks.

pineapple	pine	ap	ple	
rereading	re	read	ing	
independence	in	de	pen	dence
unforgivable	un	for	giv	a	ble

Look at each picture. Say the picture name. Write each word part by part (syllable by syllable).

ham bur ger

tel e scope

di no saur

es ca la tor

---

30 WRITING: Spelling, Grammar, and Story Structure

Relative Pronouns

Relative pronouns include **who, whose, whom, which,** and **that.** They start a clause, or group of words in a sentence, that tells more about a noun in the sentence.

Use **whose** to show ownership, or something that belongs to someone.
Whose car is in the driveway? (Someone owns the car.)

Use **who** if you can replace the word with "he."
The baker **who** won the contest is my friend. (**He** is my friend.)

Use **whom** if you can replace the word with "him." Remember: Both end with the letter **m.**
Whom did you call on the phone? (Did you call **him** on the phone?)

Use **which** if the clause (group of words) is extra information, and not necessary to understand the basic sentence. Often, you separate these words with commas (,).
Pizza, **which** is made of dough and cheese, is my favorite food. (Pizza is my favorite food.)

Use **that** if the clause (group of words) is necessary in the sentence.
The bike **that** I bought yesterday is already scratched.

Add a **pronoun** to finish each sentence.

1. The boy **who** won the contest is in my class.
2. This is the book **that** I read for my report.
3. To **whom** should I give this money?
4. **Whose** backpack is blue and has a superhero on it?

---

32 WRITING: Spelling, Grammar, and Story Structure

Progressive Verb Tense

Verbs have different tenses. Some verbs show action in the past. (I **ate** an apple for lunch.)
Some verbs show action that is happening now. (I **am reading** a book.)
Verbs that show action that is, was, or will be happening at some point in time are called **progressive verbs.** The action is ongoing, or in progress. These verbs begin with a form of the words "to be," such as **is, am, was, were,** or **will be.**

I **am** walking. (is happening)
I **was** walking. (was happening)
I **will be** walking. (will be happening)

Finish each sentence using **is, am, was, were,** or **will be.**

1. She **is/was/will be** reading a book about whales and sharks.
2. He **was** riding his bike slowly up the mountain earlier today.
3. We **will be** going on a field trip to a museum tomorrow.
4. I **am/was/will be** making a birthday cake for my grandmother.
5. They **were** listening to the concert on their phones yesterday.

---

34 WRITING: Spelling, Grammar, and Story Structure

Modal Auxiliaries

You sometimes use **helping verbs,** like can, could, may, might, and must, when writing. They are used to show a request, to show an ability, or to ask for permission.

can: Shows that a person or object is able to do something. (ability)
He **can run** very fast.

could: Shows a past ability.
She **could run** very fast.

may: Shows that someone or something is allowed to do something. It can also be used to request something.
You **may go** to the movies tomorrow. **May I go** to the movies, too?

might: Shows that something is possible or likely to happen.
The hurricane **might hit** our town at midnight.

must: Shows that something is necessary or has to happen.
You **must study** a lot for the test on Friday.

Add a **helping verb** to finish each sentence.

1. He **could** walk better before the accident.
2. You **must** help me clean up the classroom!
3. My mother **can** do more in an hour than anyone I know.
4. I **might** visit my grandparents this weekend.
5. You **may** watch TV after you do the dishes.

---

36 WRITING: Spelling, Grammar, and Story Structure

Adjective Order

Adjectives are describing words. When there is more than one adjective before a noun, they are written in a specific order: **opinion, size, condition, age, shape, color, pattern, origin, material, purpose.** Often there is a word like **a, an,** or **the** before these other words.

opinion	ugly, pretty, tasty	color	green, purple, reddish
size	large, tiny, tall	pattern	striped, zigzag, dotted
condition	dirty, wet, rich	origin	American, Asian, Spanish
age	old, young, new	material	wooden, cotton, plastic
shape	long, thin, square	purpose	shopping, riding, sleeping

Put these **adjectives** in order.

1. wooden, beautiful
   beautiful wooden table

2. yellow, old, hungry
   hungry old yellow monster

3. pretty, antique, porcelain, British
   pretty antique British porcelain plate

4. bluish, square, nice, new, striped
   nice new square bluish striped blanket

---

38 WRITING: Spelling, Grammar, and Story Structure

Prepositional Phrases

A **preposition** is a connecting word, such as **about, after, at, before, behind, by, during, for, from, in, of, over, past, to, under, up,** and **with.**
A **prepositional phrase** is a group of words in a sentence that begins with a preposition and ends with an object. The prepositional phrase does **not** contain a verb or the subject of the sentence. It gives more information about how, when, why, who, where, or which one.

We found the kitten **under the sofa.** (where)
I ate the leftover spaghetti **from last night's supper.** (when)

Circle the **prepositional phrase** in each sentence.

1. Mom told us to be quiet (during the movie).
2. The cow (from our neighbor's farm) had brown and white spots.
3. I did my homework (after our dinner).
4. Dad and I drove (to the store) to buy popcorn.

Write a sentence with each **preposition. Answers will vary**

on _____
before _____
above _____
until _____

ANSWER KEY

---

40 WRITING: Spelling, Grammar, and Story Structure

Frequently Confused Words

Some words look or sound so much alike that they can be confusing. Paying careful attention to the spellings, sounds, and meanings of these words can help you remember them. Follow these steps to learn these words.

Step 1: Read the word. Say the sounds you hear in it.
Step 2: Spell the word out loud.
Step 3: Write the word as you say the letter names.
Step 4: Think about the word's meaning. Use it in a sentence.

Use the steps to practice the words below. Check the box after completing Steps 1 and 2. Write the word for Step 3. Write a sentence for Step 4.

there (place)	Step 1 ☑ Step 2 ☑ Step 3	**there**
	Step 4	
they're (they are)	Step 1 ☑ Step 2 ☑ Step 3	**they're**
	Step 4	
their (possession)	Step 1 ☑ Step 2 ☑ Step 3	**their**
	Step 4	
your (possession)	Step 1 ☑ Step 2 ☑ Step 3	**your**
	Step 4	
you're (you are)	Step 1 ☑ Step 2 ☑ Step 3	**you're**
	Step 4	

---

42 WRITING: Spelling, Grammar, and Story Structure

Capitalization

What begins with a **capital letter**?
• the first word in a sentence
• the word **I**
• the name of a holiday, month, and exact place
• the name and title of a specific person
• the title of a book

> We eat turkey and watch football games on <u>Thanksgiving</u>.
> My family moved to <u>California</u> last <u>September</u>.
> <u>Mrs. Lee</u>, our teacher, read <u>Charlotte's Web</u> to us.

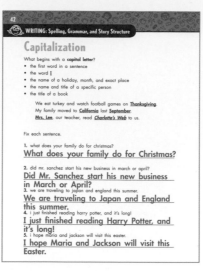

Fix each sentence.

1. what does your family do for christmas?
What does your family do for Christmas?

2. did mr. sanchez start his new business in march or april?
Did Mr. Sanchez start his new business in March or April?

3. we are traveling to japan and england this summer.
We are traveling to Japan and England this summer.

4. i just finished reading harry potter, and it's long!
I just finished reading Harry Potter, and it's long!

5. i hope maria and jackson will visit this easter.
I hope Maria and Jackson will visit this Easter.

---

44 WRITING: Spelling, Grammar, and Story Structure

Commas in Quotations

Use a **comma** to separate a direct quote and who is saying it. The comma appears **before** the quotation mark (").

> "I am not feeling well," said Tomás.
> My mother said, "You better watch out!"

Add the missing **comma** in each sentence.

1. "Don't upset me like that," yelled Olivia.

2. "I really want to be included on the team," said Marcos.

3. The hawk swooped down and screeched, "Caw! Caw!

4. Jason said, "My favorite animal is the fierce lion."

Write sentences showing what someone might say in a story. Create a conversation between two or more characters.

1. **Answers will vary**

2. _____

3. _____

4. _____

---

46 WRITING: Spelling, Grammar, and Story Structure

Quotes

Use **quotation marks** when quoting the exact words someone says.

> "I will be late to the meeting," said Mr. Chin.
> The giant screamed, "Fee, fi, fo, fum!"

Add the missing **quotation marks** in each sentence.

1. "I would really prefer pizza for my party," said the girl.
2. "We can play soccer on Saturday," said Dad.
3. "What are you dressing up as for Halloween?" asked Sophia.
4. "Run! Run!" shouted the boy. "The monster is behind you!"

Write sentences showing a conversation between you and a friend or family member.

1. **Answers will vary**

2. _____

3. _____

4. _____

---

48 WRITING: Spelling, Grammar, and Story Structure

Compound Sentences

A **compound sentence** has two sentences put together. The words **and**, **but**, **or**, and **so** are used to make a compound sentence. A comma (,) is put before one of these words.

> Ben went to the movies, **and** I stayed home to rest.
> I like to sleep late, **but** I have to get up early tomorrow.

Put together the two sentences to make a **compound sentence**.

I love gymnastics. My sister loves soccer.

I love gymnastics, and my sister loves soccer.

We like to eat chocolate. Our school doesn't allow it.

We like to eat chocolate, but our school doesn't allow it.

We can go to the park. We can go to the mall.

We can go to the park, or we can go to the mall.

---

50 WRITING: Spelling, Grammar, and Story Structure

Text Structure: Sequence

Writers of informational text use different ways to **structure** their writing. One way is to put the information in **sequence**, or **time order**.

These signal words often alert a reader that the text is organized this way: **first**, **second**, **third**, **next**, **then**, **last**, **after**, **finally**, **before**, **in the beginning**, **to start**, **meanwhile**, **in the middle**, **at the end**. The writer might also use **dates in order** (such as 1776, 1865, and 2020).

Fill in the **sequence** paragraph. Write about an interesting topic, like building or making something.

The **first** step in **Answers will vary**

is to _____

After that, you must _____

_____

Next, you need to _____

_____

Finally, you _____

_____

---

52 WRITING: Spelling, Grammar, and Story Structure

Text Structure: Cause/Effect

Writers of informational text use different ways to **structure** their writing. One way is to explain the **causes** and **effects** of something. The causes are **why** something happens. The effects are **what** happens.

These signal words often alert a reader that the text is organized this way: **because**, **cause**, **effect**, **therefore**, **if…then**, **as a result**, **due to**, **reason**, **since**, **leads to**, **as a consequence**, **consequently**.

Fill in the **cause and effect** paragraph. Write about an interesting topic, like a natural disaster or other science concept.

Because of **Answers will vary**

_____

_____ has happened.

Therefore, _____

_____

This explains why _____

_____

_____

---

54 WRITING: Spelling, Grammar, and Story Structure

Text Structure: Problem/Solution

Writers of informational text use different ways to **structure** their writing. One way is to **identify a problem** and **detail the solution** or solutions.

These signal words often alert a reader that the text is organized this way: **problem**, **solution**, **solve**, **as a result**, **consequently**, **since**, **therefore**, **because of**, **leads to**, **due to**, **as**, **then**.

Fill in the **problem and solution** paragraph. Write about an interesting topic, like an environmental issue.

The **problem** was **Answers will vary**

_____

_____

This problem happened **because** _____

_____

_____

The problem was finally **solved** when _____

_____

_____

---

56 WRITING: Spelling, Grammar, and Story Structure

Similes and Metaphors

Similes and **metaphors** are used by writers to compare things.
Similes use the words **like** or **as** to compare things.

> My cat is <u>like</u> a little tiger.
> That kitten is <u>as</u> cute <u>as</u> a button.

Metaphors directly compare things.

> Dr. Chang <u>is</u> an angel.
> Larry <u>is</u> a big chicken.

Finish each sentence using a **simile** or metaphor.

1. This winter is like **Answers will vary**

_____

2. My sister is as _____ as a

3. Our old car is like _____

4. The world is _____

5. Laughter is _____

58

Idioms

An **idiom** is a group of words that has a meaning specific to a language. This meaning is different from the actual words. For example, if a writer says, "It's raining cats and dogs," it means that it is "raining hard"—not that cats and dogs are falling from the sky.

Match the **idiom** to its meaning.

Idiom	Meaning
At the drop of a hat	A great idea or plan
The ball is in your court	It is up to you to take the next step or to do something
Barking up the wrong tree	Right away; instantly
Best thing since sliced bread	You are teasing me
You're pulling my leg	It is very expensive
Costs an arm and a leg	Looking in the wrong place or accusing the wrong person of something
Feel a bit under the weather	You're exactly right
Hit the nail on the head	Someone is sick

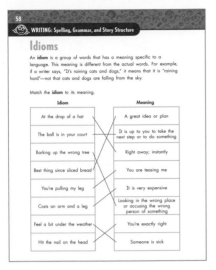

60

Characters and Settings

The **characters** are whom the story is about. We learn about characters from what they say, think, and do. We also learn about them from what other characters say about them.
The **setting** is where and when a story takes place.

Fill in the chart using information from your favorite stories.

Story:	Answers will vary
Setting:	
Main Character:	
What You Know About the Character and How:	

Story:	Answers will vary
Setting:	
Main Character:	
What You Know About the Character and How:	

62

Point of View

Point of view is how a story is told. It affects the information the reader gets from the story's narrator—the person telling the story.

First Person Point of View: The narrator, or person telling the story, is **in** the story. Key words used are **I** and **my**. We "hear" and "see" the story through the narrator's eyes only. Therefore, the information the narrator can provide is limited.

Second Person Point of View: The narrator is speaking directly to the reader, using words like **you** or **your**. Few stories are told in this way.

Third Person Point of View: The narrator, or person telling the story, is **not** in the story. We "hear" and "see" the story from an outside voice.

Fill in the chart using information from your favorite stories.

Story:	Answers will vary	
Point of View:		How You Know:

Story:	Answers will vary	
Point of View:		How You Know:

64

Prefixes

A **prefix** is a word part added to the beginning of a word. It changes the meaning of the word.

un, dis = not or the opposite of
re = again
mis = bad, wrong, incorrectly

happy	**un**happy	(not happy)
like	**dis**like	(the opposite of like)
read	**re**read	(read again)
treat	**mis**treat	(treat badly or wrongly)

Add **un, dis, re,** or **mis** to finish each word.

dis/reappear   **un**friendly
disobey   **un/dis**able
misunderstood   **un/re**make
unclear   **re**play
dis/reapprove   **dis/mis/re**place

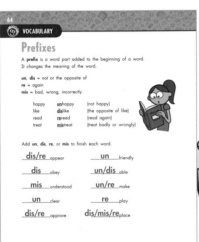

66

Prefixes

A **prefix** is a word part added to the beginning of a word. It changes the meaning of the word.

pre = before
sub = under or below
mid = halfway or middle point
super = above, beyond
ir = not

read	**pre**read	(read before)
way	**sub**way	(pathway under the surface)
day	**mid**day	(middle of the day)
human	**super**human	(beyond human)
regular	**ir**regular	(not regular)

Add **pre, sub, mid, super,** or **ir** to finish each word.

precook   **pre/mid**game
supernatural   **pre**write
irresponsible   **sub**freezing
preplan   **super**star
mid/subway   **ir**replaceable

68

Suffixes

A **suffix** is a word part added to the end of a word. It changes the meaning of the word. Sometimes the spelling of the base word changes when the suffix is added.

ful = full of, with
less = without, not
y, ous = full of

care	care**ful**	(full of care)
fear	fear**less**	(without fear)
rain	rain**y**	(full of rain)
poison	poison**ous**	(full of poison)

Add **ful, less, y,** or **ous** to finish each word.

storm**y**   weight**less/y**
doubt**ful/less**   grass**y**
humor**less/ous**   hope**ful/less**
health**ful/y**   odor**less/ous**
use**ful/less**   need**less/y**

70

Suffixes

A **suffix** is a word part added to the end of a word. It changes the meaning of the word. Sometimes the spelling of the base word changes when the suffix is added.

ment, tion/ion = state of being (forms a noun)
ly = in a certain way
ness = quality or state of

amaze	amaze**ment**	(state of being amazed)
correct	correc**tion**	(state of being correct)
slow	slow**ly**	(in a slow way)
happy	happi**ness**	(state of being happy)

Add **ment, tion/ion, ly,** or **ness** to finish each word.

eager**ly/ness**   embarrass**ment**
dark**ly/ness**   rare**ly/ness**
equip**ment**   act**ion**
achieve**ment**   friend**ly**
predict**ion**   ill**ness**

72

Latin Roots

Some roots, such as **port, scrib/script,** and **spect,** come from Latin. That's a language that was spoken long ago. You can use the root to figure out the meaning of the word.

Root	Meaning
port	carry
scrib/script	write
spect	see/look

Put together the parts of each word and write them below.

ex + port = **export**
scrib + ble = **scribble**
spect + a + tor = **spectator**
im + port = **import**
pre + script + ion = **prescription**
in + spect = **inspect**

Write a definition for three of the words above, using the **root** as a clue.

Word	Definition
Answers will vary	

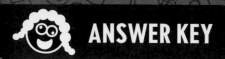
ANSWER KEY

74 VOCABULARY
Latin Roots

Some roots, such as **struct**, **ven/vent**, and **vid/vis**, come from Latin. That's a language that was spoken long ago.
You can use the root to figure out the meaning of the word.

Root	Meaning
struct	build
ven/vent	come
vid/vis	see

Put together the parts of each word and write them below.

con + struct + ion = **construction**
con + vene = **convene**
vis + u + al + ize = **visualize**
de + struct + ion = **destruction**
con + ven + tion = **convention**
in + vis + ible = **invisible**

Write a definition for three of the words above, using the **root** as a clue.

Word — Definition
Answers will vary

76 VOCABULARY
Greek Roots

Some roots, such as **bio**, **graph**, **phon**, **auto**, **tri**, and **oct**, come from Greek. That's a language that was spoken long ago. It's still spoken today. You can use the root to figure out the meaning of the word.

Root	Meaning
bio	life
graph	write
phon	sound/hear
auto	self
tri	three
oct	eight

Put together the parts of each word and write them below.
bio + graph + y = **biography**
micro + phone = **microphone**
oct + opus = **octopus**
auto + graph = **autograph**
tri + angle = **triangle**

Write a definition for three of the words above, using the **root** as a clue.
Word — Definition
Answers will vary

78 VOCABULARY
Greek Roots

Some roots, such as **geo**, **scope**, **tele**, **photo**, **astro**, and **therm**, come from Greek. That's a language that was spoken long ago. It's still spoken today. You can use the root to figure out the meaning of the word.

Root	Meaning
geo	earth
scope	see/look/examine
tele	far/distant
photo	light
astro	star
therm	heat

Put together the parts of each word and write them below.
geo + logy = **geology**
tele + scope = **telescope**
astro + logy = **astrology**
therm + o + meter = **thermometer**
photo + synthesis = **photosynthesis**

Write a definition for three of the words above, using the **root** as a clue.
Word — Definition
Answers will vary

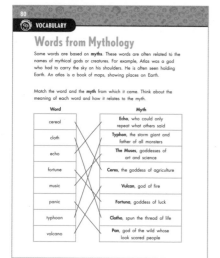

80 VOCABULARY
Words from Mythology

Some words are based on **myths**. These words are often related to the names of mythical gods or creatures. For example, Atlas was a god who had to carry the sky on his shoulders. He is often seen holding Earth. An atlas is a book of maps, showing places on Earth.

Match the word and the **myth** from which it came. Think about the meaning of each word and how it relates to the myth.

Word	Myth
cereal	Echo, who could only repeat what others said
cloth	Typhon, the storm giant and father of all monsters
echo	The Muses, goddesses of art and science
fortune	Ceres, the goddess of agriculture
music	Vulcan, god of fire
panic	Fortuna, goddess of luck
typhoon	Clotho, spun the thread of life
volcano	Pan, god of the wild whose look scared people

82 VOCABULARY
Shades of Meaning: Adjectives

Adjectives are describing words. Some adjectives mean almost the same thing. However, each adjective has a slightly different meaning.

large (big)
giant (very big)
enormous (very, very big)

Add an **adjective** to finish each sentence: **angry, furious, happy, ecstatic**.

1. We were **ecstatic** when we won the gold medal after years of trying.
2. He was **furious** that the most important game of the year was canceled.
3. She was **angry** that she had a hole in her sock.
4. I was **happy** to play at the beach all day.

Write a sentence with each word: **good, wonderful, phenomenal**.
1. **Answers will vary**
2.
3.

84 VOCABULARY
Shades of Meaning: Verbs

Verbs are action words. Some verbs mean almost the same thing. However, each verb has a slightly different meaning.

nibbled (ate by taking little bites)
ate (ate normally)
devoured (ate quickly)

Add a **verb** to finish each sentence: **fell, collapsed, strolled, trudged**.

1. He **collapsed** after running in the scorching heat.
2. We **strolled** along the beach one evening.
3. She tripped and **fell** on the sidewalk.
4. He **trudged** to the principal's office to get his punishment.

Write a sentence with each word: **look, peek, gaze**.
1. **Answers will vary**
2.
3.

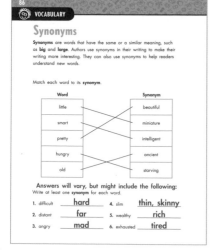

86 VOCABULARY
Synonyms

Synonyms are words that have the same or a similar meaning, such as **big** and **large**. Authors use synonyms in their writing to make their writing more interesting. They can also use synonyms to help readers understand new words.

Match each word to its **synonym**.

Word	Synonym
little	beautiful
smart	miniature
pretty	intelligent
hungry	ancient
old	starving

Answers will vary, but might include the following:
Write at least one **synonym** for each word.
1. difficult **hard**
2. distant **far**
3. angry **mad**
4. slim **thin, skinny**
5. wealthy **rich**
6. exhausted **tired**

88 VOCABULARY
Antonyms

Antonyms are words that have the opposite meaning, such as **big** and **small**. Authors use antonyms in their writing to make their writing more interesting.

Match each word to its **antonym**.

Word	Antonym
tiny	young
pretty	easy
ancient	huge
difficult	unattractive
furious	thrilled

Answers will vary, but might include the following:
Write at least one **antonym** for each word.
1. energetic **tired**
2. rich **poor**
3. distant **near**
4. quiet **loud**
5. strong **weak**
6. hardworking **lazy**

90 VOCABULARY
Context Clues

Authors sometimes give clues to help a reader figure out the meaning of a new word. We call these **context clues**. There are many types of context clues. Here are a few:

Definition or Restatement: a definition of the word is given right after it, often in parentheses or followed by **is** or **means**
Synonym: a word with a similar meaning is given, often using the words **or, that is,** or **which is**
Example: lists of related things are given, and the word is often followed by **such as, include, these,** or **for example**
Word Part Clue: the reader can use prefixes, suffixes, and roots to figure out the meaning of the word

Read the sentence, focusing on the **boldfaced** word. Write the type of **context clue** given to help figure out its meaning.

1. **synonym** The **miniature**, or really small, insect could barely be seen.
2. **definition** The car **accelerated** at a fast rate. Accelerate means to speed up.

Write a sentence for one of these words: **observe, demolish, ginormous, evolve**. Provide a context clue to help your reader.
Answers will vary